IMAGES
of America

ROCKY MOUNTAIN
NATIONAL PARK

Pictured here are Fern Lake, Notchtop Mountain, and the Little Matterhorn by ranger Al Rozum. Just across from the Moraine Park Museum in Rocky Mountain National Park is a 3-mile road leading to the Fern Lake trailhead. The elevation at the trailhead is 8,155 feet. The first part of the trail is nice and flat through ferns and parallels Big Thompson Creek. Then it begins a series of switchbacks. A walk of 2.5 miles leads to Fern Falls that plunges 60 feet amid a jumble of downed timber. The hike all the way to beautiful Fern Lake is 3.8 miles. In the background of this picture, Notchtop Mountain is to the left and the Little Matterhorn to the right. The Little Matterhorn reaches a height of 11,586 feet. Notchtop Mountain has an elevation of 12,129 feet, and its true summit is a technical climb.

ON THE COVER: A mountaineer rappels down this steep side of rock in the Eagle Cliff area of Rocky Mountain National Park. Eagle Cliff Mountain is near the Beaver Meadows Park entrance. This photograph, taken by Roger Contor, geologist and former park superintendent, on August 23, 1963, shows one of many exciting climbs available to qualified visitors to the park. (Courtesy Rocky Mountain National Park archives.)

IMAGES
of America

ROCKY MOUNTAIN NATIONAL PARK

Phyllis J. Perry

ARCADIA
PUBLISHING

Copyright © 2008 by Phyllis J. Perry
ISBN 978-0-7385-5627-7

Published by Arcadia Publishing
Charleston, South Carolina

Printed in the United States of America

Library of Congress Catalog Card Number: 2007941878

For all general information contact Arcadia Publishing at:
Telephone 843-853-2070
Fax 843-853-0044
E-mail sales@arcadiapublishing.com
For customer service and orders:
Toll-Free 1-888-313-2665

Visit us on the Internet at www.arcadiapublishing.com

To David L. Perry, who has hiked, backpacked, snowshoed, cross-country skied, and shared his love and knowledge of this park with friends and three generations of family.

All photographs are courtesy of Rocky Mountain National Park, National Park Service.

CONTENTS

ACKNOWLEDGMENTS

The Rocky Mountain National Park archives of historic photographs proved to be a treasure trove of striking images, capturing and preserving vivid moments in time and providing a remarkable pictorial history of this area before and after it was designated a national park. All the images used in the book came from the Rocky Mountain National Park archives, National Park Service.

I am especially indebted to Tim Burchett, museum curator, Rocky Mountain National Park, for his assistance and for his patience in explaining to me how to access this vast collection using its unique filing system. I am also appreciative of the help given by Larry Frederick, chief of interpretation and education at Rocky Mountain National Park; Joan Childers, park ranger, Division of Interpretation; Kathy Brown, ranger; Ken Unitt, information technology specialist; and museum volunteer Kathy Levine, for their help in various ways on this project. Finally, I am most grateful to my husband, David L. Perry, who assisted at every step of the journey, from finding and selecting images to scanning them and commenting on the text.

I also want to thank my editor at Arcadia Publishing, Hannah Carney, for entrusting this special project to me and providing expert guidance.

INTRODUCTION

Rocky Mountain National Park, located in north-central Colorado astride the Continental Divide, is a breathtaking place. Woodrow Wilson signed the law establishing it as a national park on January 26, 1915. Its more than 415 square miles feature lush valleys and showcase the grandeur of the Rocky Mountains with Longs Peak towering at 14,259 feet.

After a stop at one of the visitor centers, some will drive through the park, admiring the spectacular views and glimpses of wildlife, the wildflowers so abundant in summer, or the golden aspen that glow in autumn. They may be fortunate enough to approach or leave the park via Trail Ridge Road, on which construction began in 1926. Eight miles of this spectacular highway in the sky are above 11,000 feet with one amazing view after another around each curve.

Other visitors may be lucky enough to stay for several days in one of the five drive-in campgrounds or more than 200 backcountry campsites that the park boasts. For those who have time to explore, there are 359 miles of trails for hikers, backpackers, and horseback riders to enjoy in spring, summer, and fall. Anglers can fish many of the streams and lakes. Bird-watchers will be busy spotting everything from songbirds and magpies to eagles and hawks. And photographers will come away with pictures of mule deer, moose, bighorn sheep, black bears, coyotes, and cougars. Some hardy visitors will climb peaks. Others who come in winter will enjoy snowshoeing or cross-country skiing.

The park is rich in history that includes Native Americans; homesteaders; early commercial activities such as mining, logging, and hunting; colorful and demanding construction projects like building Trail Ridge Road, the work of the Civilian Conservation Corps, and the creation of the Alva Adams tunnel; and tales of danger and adventure, including lightning strikes, floods, fire, and daring mountain rescues. All who are introduced to this "crown jewel" of the park system will be entranced with Rocky Mountain National Park.

Trail Ridge Road covers 48 miles between Estes Park on Rocky Mountain National Park's east side and Grand Lake on the west. Travelers in either direction climb 4,000 feet in less than an hour. Eleven miles of the highway are above tree line. The road winds through a vast tundra to its high point at 12,183 feet in elevation. It is the highest continuous paved motor highway in the world.

This 1974 view shows the West Side Headquarters and Kawuneechee Visitor Center. This center and the Beaver Meadows Visitor Center are open every day all year. Other places of interest that open seasonally at various times include the Fall River Visitor Center, Alpine Visitor Center, Lily Lake Visitor Center, Moraine Park Museum, Holzwarth Historic Site, Bear Lake kiosk, and Sheep Lakes and Corral Creek information stations.

One

NATIVE AMERICANS
IN THE AREA

Scholars believe migrating people who were hunters crossing from Asia to North America gradually moved southward into the Rocky Mountain National Park area 10,000 to 15,000 years ago. Mammoth remains and projectile points were unearthed just 35 miles east of the park at the Dent archeological site. About 45 miles northeast of the park is the Lindenmeier site, which archeologists believe was an ancient Folsom camping spot about 11,000 years ago. Four Clovis and Folsom projectile points have been found in the park. Alpine campsites south of the park reveal large game drive systems that date between 3850 and 3400 B.C.

These sites suggest early Native Americans did not remain all year but came seasonally to hunt and migrated to warmer elevations in winter. What is now Trail Ridge Road was a usable east-west route for crossing the mountains. Close to Trail Ridge road is a stone wall structure that permitted hunters to direct game animals toward men waiting with weapons. Between A.D. 400 and 650, bows and arrows were used. In addition to mountain animals, these Native Americans ate berries, currants, and roots.

Ute, Arapaho, and Cheyenne were among the tribes that came into the Rocky Mountain Park area. The Ute were mentioned as being in the southern Rocky Mountains as early as 1626, and the Arapaho and Cheyenne came into Colorado around 1800. They all ranged in Colorado during the 19th century in the area of Estes Park, Grand Lake, and the land that is now Rocky Mountain National Park. They were seen by early settlers, and they left signs of having lived here or passed through. While the Arapaho and Cheyenne hunted mainly on the plains of eastern Colorado, the Ute remained in the western part of the state and ranged into central Utah. There was a deadly enmity between the Ute and the other two groups. Well-worn trails, a few teepee rings, bits of pottery, arrow points, some tools, and pieces of hunting equipment are the remains of these Native Americans in the park area.

Ute and Arapaho used passes and trails in what is now Rocky Mountain National Park as ways to catch enemies by surprise and as places to hunt deer, elk, and other game. Occasionally a Native American came to a high country location to catch an eagle. Eagles were valued for their decorative feathers. Only certain men of the tribe were chosen for this task, and they prepared themselves by fasting for four days before putting medicine on their hands and going on their eagle hunt. This drawing shows an eagle trap. The hunter would dig a pit in which to hide, conceal it with a pile of brush, and place a piece of meat on top to lure the eagle. Tales were told of trapping eagles on Longs Peak, but the first recorded climbers of the peak found no evidence of this in 1868.

In 1937, ranger Jack Moomaw took this picture revealing a site on Mount Ida that was part of a Native American game drive. The hunters constructed these rock walls to enhance the natural contour of the slopes. Some hunters would frighten and drive the game animals toward spots where other tribe members lay in wait with weapons such as spears that were tipped with sharp stone points.

These are the remains of a Native American game wall along Tombstone Ridge. Constructing these stone game walls took considerable time and effort, but they were no doubt used repeatedly by Native American hunters. Mountain sheep, mule deer, and elk were among the available game. Sometimes the walls had a U or V shape to funnel the animals toward waiting hunters.

This close-up of the remains of a game wall close to Trail Ridge Road was taken by ranger Dorr G. Yeager in 1933. Some stone walls have been discovered that stretch for hundreds of feet in length. It is likely that about two dozen people were needed to drive the sheep or elk and to attack the animals in ambush.

A hunting blind near Iron Dike that was used by Native Americans is shown in this photograph. When they were first discovered, it was thought that these stone piles were some sort of fortifications that warriors used to defend their territory. Later it was decided that these were typical devices used by hunters in other arctic or tundra environments where the country is devoid of cover.

This path, known as the Ute Trail, crosses the Continental Divide. The Ute and Comanche had a falling out, and by 1755, the Ute had retreated back to the western slope of the Rockies. Once or twice a year, the Ute returned to hunt on the Great Plains. They used several trails, passes, saddles, and canyons to cross the Front Range.

Not far from the Thompson River is this teepee ring. Native Americans who used the park area were nomadic. They did not rely upon crops but moved often to hunt or gather food. They hunted buffalo, elk, deer, and antelope and snared jackrabbits. They did not build permanent houses. Instead they lived in bison-hide tipis, which could be taken down and moved, or in brush-covered wickiups.

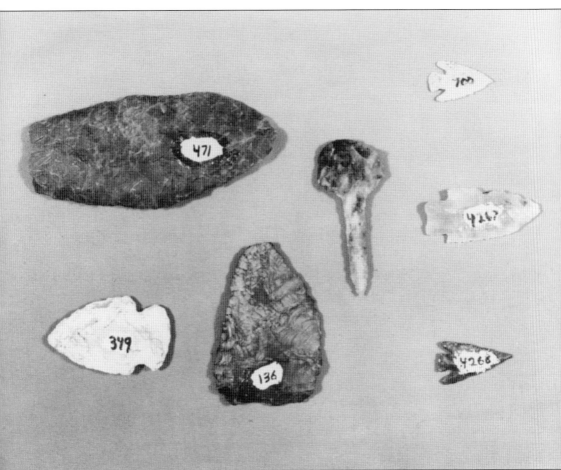

Pictures of the tools shown here were taken by park naturalist Wayne Alcorn. A variety of sharpened stones were used by Native Americans in hunting and in other tasks. Arrows, axes, and lances were used to kill game. Sharpened stones might be used to polish bone antlers. Hard, smooth, fine-grained stones such as flint, chert, chalcedony, and agate were used for tools. Men of the tribe were the hunters and warriors, while women did the cooking, prepared and tanned deerskins used for making clothing, and did other tasks. The main diet of Native Americans such as the Arapaho was meat. They especially relied on the successful hunting of buffalo, elk, and deer, which they cooked in pots or dried into strips of jerky.

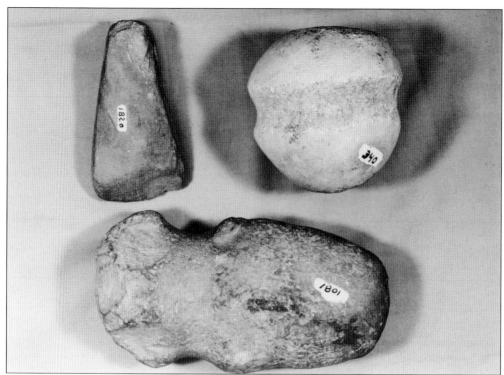

Large rocks could be used as hammers and to crush seeds. Sharpened stones were also used to skin the hide from a deer and to cut and scrape hides. In Ute society, the man had the responsibility for hunting and care of the horses. For variety, they added fruits and roots which they collected to their diet.

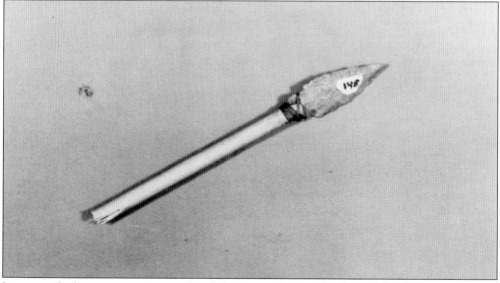

Lances with sharp stone points predated the bow and arrow by thousands of years. To make a spear or arrow head, a piece was flaked off of a larger smooth, fine-grained stone. Breaking along controlled lines yielded razor-sharp flakes. Smaller pieces were shaped and sharpened with a bone tool while using a leather hand guard.

This 1914 photograph shows a small group of Arapaho who were invited to the park to consult regarding their memories of place names in the area. Tom Crispin acted as interpreter, and Shep Husted guided their pack trip through the park. Oliver Toll recorded their observations in a book entitled *Arapaho Names and Trails*. This visit was organized by Harriet Vaille on behalf of the Colorado Geographical Society. The society had requested that the U.S. Geological Survey hold off printing names on a map of the area until they had a chance to capture the names used for these features by Native Americans who lived here in the past. As a result, many features in the park and surrounding area now bear Native American names such as Mount Neota ("mountain sheep's heart") and Nokhu Crags ("rocks where the eagles nest"). The valley of the North Fork of the Grand River became Kawuneechee ("coyote") Valley. This section of the country has the greatest concentration of such names in any part of the United States.

The Kawuneechee Valley of Rocky Mountain National Park takes its name from the Arapaho word for "coyote." This valley and the Never Summer Range form the western boundary of Rocky Mountain National Park. In the late 1870s, many prospectors for gold and silver came through this area to establish the boom towns of Lulu City, Gaskill, and Dutchtown. Because this side of the park gets more rain and snow than the eastern side, it contains lush forests and swollen streams. Abundant in the area are beaver, amphibians, otters, and mountain birds. The mighty Colorado River, which runs 1,450 miles to the Gulf of California, begins as a swift stream at the northern end of the Kawuneechee Valley. Since 1988, after a reintroduction program, moose have become well established again in this habitat, and in October and November, bull elk bugle to their herds in the Kawuneechee Valley.

Two

HOMESTEADERS, CABINS, AND LODGES

The mountains admired today in Rocky Mountain National Park were the very reason that people did not settle into this area as early as they did other parts of the state. These huge mountains were barriers. Trappers and traders followed trails and streams in the Rockies starting about 1811. Official explorers such as Maj. Stephen H. Long led an expedition to the base of the Rockies in 1820. In 1843, Rufus B. Sage was one of the first men to actually write about the fur trappers in this area.

When the 1849 California Gold Rush was followed 10 years later by strikes in Colorado, fifty-niners poured in. Towns such as Denver and mining camps like Black Hawk and Central City sprang up. Joel Estes left his farm in Missouri to seek gold in California and Oregon. Hearing of strikes in Colorado, he brought his family to Denver. After exploring the area now known as Estes Park, he decided to homestead and raise cattle. In 1859 and 1860, Estes and two of his sons built two log cabins at the eastern end of what is now the park, where they raised cattle and sold meat to hungry prospectors.

A few others settled in the area at the same time. The trapper Philip Crenshaw built his cabin near Grand Lake around 1858. Alonzo Allen, a gold seeker, built a cabin southeast of Longs Peak in 1864. Cold winters and the isolation led Joel Estes to move to better ranching country in southern Colorado in 1866. Editor William N. Byers of the Rocky Mountain News was an outdoorsman who had visited Estes's cabin. Though unsuccessful in trying to climb Longs Peak, Byers wrote glowing stories of the area. In addition to ranching, people began to see its possibilities as a summer resort for hikers, climbers, hunters, fishermen, and vacationers to enjoy the mountain air and scenery. Word spread. The spectacular area around what is now Rocky Mountain National Park was "discovered," and a diverse group of people started moving in.

STORY OF THE FIRST HOME

JOEL ESTES

The first cabin was built by Joel Estes and his son Milton in the fall of 1859. The following year a larger cabin was constructed on the site of the present ranch house at the junction of the Fish Creek, Lyons, and Loveland roads. To this, in 1860, Joel brought his wife and it served as the family home until the Estes left in 1866. In 1861 Milton brought Mary Flemming to the cabin as his bride and their son Charles who arrived in 1865, was the first white child born in the park.

The life of the Estes family was one of simplicity. Meals consisted of wild meats supplemented by breads and were prepared in fireplace kettles and Dutch ovens. Eagle wings are said to have served for brooms, and pitch pine burned in the fireplace for light. Biannual trips to Denver sufficed to supply their scanty needs and to secure the mail. Their first visitors came after three years when some campers wandered into the region.

The cabin in which the family lived was a long, low building. It passed into several hands after the Estes vacated, and sometime between 1868 and 1873 Griff Evans, then the owner, improved it and added a gable.

This picture of a plaque placed to mark the site of Joes Estes's cabin on Fish Creek was taken in 1935. It commemorates the first home built in the area. With the help of his son Milton, Joel Estes built a cabin in 1859 and the following year built a second, larger one. He raised cattle in this meadow, or park, and also hunted big game to sell in Denver.

John C. Preston, park ranger, took this photograph of the old Joel Estes homestead in 1935. It was an isolated, long, low building. Milton Estes brought his bride, Mary Flemming, to live in the cabin in 1861, and their son, Charles, was the first white child born in the park. According to reports, the Estes family lived in the home for three years before receiving their first visitors.

At age 28, William N. Byers arrived in Denver in April 1859. Just six days later, Denver's first newspaper, the *Rocky Mountain News*, hit the street. Byers had been born in Ohio in 1831, moved to Iowa, and then gone to Nebraska where he worked as a surveyor. With no journalistic training, he saw opportunity in the Colorado gold rush. He decided to move to Denver and establish a newspaper, although Denver and Auraria between them at that time had less than 1,000 residents. Byers bought an old printing press in Iowa, loaded it on a wagon, and made a 42-day trip to the Rockies through spring snows. He set up his press in a rickety building above a saloon and began publication. A great outdoorsman, Byers enjoyed the area. After founding the paper, Byers ran it until 1878. As editor of the city's first newspaper, Byers became a member of a group of powerful Denver leaders.

Due to growing interest in the American West following the Civil War, Congress funded several geographical and topographical expeditions. Photographer William Henry Jackson took this picture of Dr. Ferdinand Vandiveer Hayden in his camp near Golden, Colorado, in 1872. Hayden led the U.S. Geographical Survey of the territories. Gathering the data meant hauling triangulation equipment to the top of peaks to determine distance and elevation measurements.

Photographer William Henry Jackson took this picture in 1874 of Dr. F. V. Hayden, survey leader, on one of his Colorado surveying expeditions. In addition to making careful maps and geologic charts of the area and using barometers to calculate elevations, some survey members also noted details of flora and fauna and even described existing mining camps.

This picture of William Henry Jackson was taken in 1873. Jackson was sometimes referred to as the "photographer of the west." He took the first photographs of the Ancient Puebloan ruins at Mesa Verde in addition to views of Longs Peak and other dramatic scenes in the Rocky Mountains. Jackson recorded his panoramas on fragile glass plates using bulky camera equipment.

As reports about the American West began to reach the general public, visitors flocked into the area that is now Rocky Mountain National Park. Some came to hunt, others to climb, and some to simply look. These cabins, belonging to Griff Evans, rented for $8 a week, providing rooms and food for tourists. Evans operated Colorado's first dude ranch in 1872 and supplied horses and guide services.

Isabella Lucy Bird was born in Yorkshire, England, in 1831. Due to poor health, she was advised to travel. Bird had already made trips to Canada and the eastern part of the United States when she came to the Rocky Mountain National Park area of Colorado in 1873. She immediately determined to climb Longs Peak even though she was not really equipped to do so. Griff Evans advised her that it was too late in the season and that snows might come at any time. Bird prevailed upon another early settler, James Nugent, better known as "Rocky Mountain Jim," to guide her to the top of the peak. He half-carried and half-pulled her to the mountain top and down again. Bird wrote many letters to her sister, which she later gathered together and published in her book, *A Lady's Life in the Rocky Mountains*, describing her three months of adventures. Bird summed up her Rocky Mountain visit by writing, "This is surely one of the most entrancing spots on earth."

The Hupp family homestead, built on the slope of Deer Mountain in lower Beaver Meadows, is shown in this 1875 photograph. John T. and Eliza Hupp built a three-room log-and-frame home and later a rear addition. They also built stables, a root cellar, chicken house, and milk house. The Hupps, with their seven children, kept a herd of 50 cattle and grew vegetables, potatoes, hay, barley, and wheat.

Wyndham Thomas Wyndham-Quin, the Irish Earl of Dunraven, came to hunt in the Estes Park area in 1872. Returning in 1873, he started buying land for a private game preserve. He established a company to purchase claims staked by men under the Homestead Law. The earl built this ranch, and his company soon owned 8,200 acres. He eventually sold the land under angry pressure from legitimate homesteaders.

This is a picture of the English Hotel in the 1890s. The Earl of Dunraven asked the artist Albert Bierstadt to select a site for his new hotel. Bierstadt chose a spot on the eastern side of Estes Park near Fish Creek. In 1877, work began on the Estes Park Hotel, which locally was called the English Hotel. It opened to the public in the summer of 1877.

Pictured here is a rodeo held for the entertainment of guests at the English Hotel. In a short period of time, this Rocky Mountain area changed from scattered primitive ranches to a widely publicized resort with accommodations for tourists. In describing the setting of his new first-class hotel, the Earl of Dunraven boasted "the marks of carriage wheels are more plentiful than elk signs."

Rev. Elkanah Lamb came to Colorado as a United Brethren minister riding on horseback to visit his parishioners. Lamb gave up missionary work and built a home at the base of Longs Peak for his family in 1875. In addition to farming, he established a lodge for visitors called Longs Peak House. Lamb and his son, Carlyle, guided people up and down Longs Peak, charging $5 a trip.

Lamb chose a beautiful spot for his Estes Park homestead in 1875. He and his son constructed a 12-by-14-foot cabin and gradually added buildings. While some settlers were quick to sell their land to the Earl of Dunraven, others resisted. Elkanah Lamb said those who cooperated with the earl were "prepared to sell their souls for a mess of pottage at the dictation of a foreign lord."

In 1885, this picture was taken of Lamb's East Longs Peak Hotel. In September of that year, an early snow fell in the park area to a depth of 2 feet. It proved to be a particularly difficult winter with periodic blizzards that persisted through late spring. On May 20, a final blizzard arrived that lasted 36 hours. It dumped 3 feet of snow in the region.

F. E. Chapin captured this photograph of Mills Glacier Snowfield on Longs Peak in 1888. When Rev. Elkanah Lamb climbed to the top of Longs Peak in 1871 and decided to come down the east side, he created a way no one had ever used before. His precipitous path of slipping, sliding, and clinging is to this day called Lambs Slide, the upper narrow snow slope shown in this picture.

This 1889 photograph taken by F. E. Chapin shows Reverend Lamb's son, Carlyle, at Mills Moraine. Carlyle guided many visitors to the top of Longs Peak. One such trip ended in disaster. While they were descending the peak, a pistol carried in the pocket of one of the climbers discharged, sending a bullet through the boy's neck. Although Lamb hurried for help, the boy bled to death on the Longs Peak summit.

Many people worked hard to have the land around Estes Park set aside as a national park, including Enos Abijah Mills, often called the "Father of Rocky Mountain National Park." Mills was born in Fort Scott, Kansas, in 1870. Because of poor health, he moved to Colorado when he was 14. He worked at various jobs, including at Elkhorn Lodge and Lamb's Ranch and as a guide up Longs Peak.

Mills was a loner during his early years in the park area, whether hiking on his own or serving as a Colorado state snow observer, measuring the depth of snow to predict spring and summer runoff. But a friend gave Mills a border collie pup named Scotch in 1902, and Scotch became a faithful companion. He was the only pet allowed at Longs Peak Inn, where he would join guests on their nature hikes. Scotch is credited with saving the life of a solo climber who reached the summit of a mountain so late in the day that she couldn't get back down before nightfall. Scotch stayed with her, helping keep her alive during a freezing night, until a rescue party reached them.

Soon after arriving in the Estes Park area, Mills claimed a site across Tahosa Creek from Lamb's Ranch and started building a cabin. This 1914 photograph of Enos Mills shows him standing in the door of his cabin, where he did much of his writing. He wrote 17 books and hundreds of articles about the Rocky Mountain National Park area.

In 1902, Enos Mills bought the ranch from Lamb, his father's cousin, and renamed it Longs Peak Inn. He encouraged people at his guesthouse to walk, climb, and enjoy the beauties of nature. This picture shows Mills with climbers on Longs Peak. A 1906 fire destroyed the main lodge, and Mills rebuilt it according to his own specifications. After Mills's death in 1922, his widow, Esther, ran the inn.

Enos Mills is pictured at the top of Longs Peak with eight-year-old Harriet Peters. Two years earlier, Mills had promised the little girl that he would guide her up the mountain when she was big enough. One September morning in 1905, the two of them set out on horseback, tied off their horses at about 11,000 feet, and continued on foot. According to Mills's account, Harriet needed very little help. Sometimes she led while most of the time she followed him. When they reached the part of the climb called the Homestretch, where many adults resort to climbing along on their hands and knees, Harriet walked upright, swinging her arms as she went. It took them only five hours to climb to the summit. In describing this climb, Mills wrote, "Of the two hundred and fifty-odd trips which I made as a guide to the summit of this great old peak, the trip with Harriet is the one I like best to recall."

Abner Sprague grew up in Dundee, Illinois, and came to Colorado in 1864 when he was 14 years old. He went to work as a locating engineer for the Missouri Pacific Railroad. By 1875, Sprague had journeyed to the area near Estes Park and claimed some land adjacent to the property owned by the Earl of Dunraven's land company.

Abner Sprague chose a spot to build by a spring in Moraine Park. Soon after filing a homestead claim in May 1875, Sprague constructed a 24-by-16-foot log cabin. Other relatives also staked claims nearby totaling 640 acres. Sprague had originally intended to ranch and farm, though he later decided to take advantage of a booming tourist business. Pictured here is Abner's wife, Alberta, feeding her chickens.

The Earl of Dunraven's land was managed by Theodore Whyte, who tried to force other homesteaders out of the region. Whyte rounded up the earl's cattle and drove them onto Sprague's land. Sprague drove the earl's cattle back to Estes Park. When this happened a second time, Sprague held a heated discussion with Whyte and had no further trouble with him. This photograph shows Sprague on horseback.

Although he continued with his ranching, Thomas Sprague soon entered the tourist industry. First he added a number of rustic log cabins to his property for guests whom he entertained at various outdoor activities, including hiking and horseback riding. Then he built a main lodge containing guest rooms, a kitchen, and a dining room.

After Sprague sold his original ranch to James Stead, he and his wife moved to Loveland but could not stay away from the Estes Park area. They moved back to another property in Glacier Basin for which Sprague held a lease from the forest service. Here in 1914, they reentered the resort business by opening a new guest facility called Sprague's Lodge.

Abner and Alberta Sprague were supportive partners, first at Sprague Ranch in Moraine Park and later at the Sprague's Lodge in Glacier Basin, where they expanded a log cabin they had built for vacation use into a two-story lodge for tourists, complete with a trout lake, now known as Sprague Lake. In 1916, it was enlarged again. Abner named a waterfall in Glacier Gorge for his wife.

MacGregor Ranch, a 160-acre claim homesteaded by Alexander MacGregor in 1874, is located at the mouth of the Black Canyon. MacGregor erected several buildings and also constructed a toll road from Lyons to Estes Park that was opened for use in July 1875. To accommodate visitors, the MacGregors built cabins and a dining hall on the north side of Black Canyon Creek.

Clara and Alexander MacGregor met in Colorado in 1872. She had come on a sketching trip with an art instructor, and he was a new Denver lawyer. Instead of forming a law firm with Judge Westbrook Decker, MacGregor married Clara and they came to Estes Park to take up ranching and farming. Pictured here are Alexander, Clara, and their three sons in 1893.

When a post office was to be established in the town of Estes Park in 1876, MacGregor offered one of his buildings at the ranch for that use. It became the first post office with Clara MacGregor as the postmistress. This is a view of Longs Peak from MacGregor's Ranch taken by park superintendent Edmund B. Rogers. Today it is a working ranch, youth education center, and museum.

Elkanah Lamb opened Wind River Lodge to guests in 1902. After Enos Mills bought Longs Peak House from the Lambs, the elder Lambs moved to their other property, 160 acres of land just to the northeast. This land was sold by the Lambs in 1911 and resold several times since then. It is now the Wind River Ranch.

Abner Sprague's sister, Arah, was the first teacher at Namaqua, a small settlement on the Big Thompson River. Arah married Alson Chapman in 1876, and they had two sons. When her husband died, Arah and her sons moved to Moraine Park, and they built the Chapman Ranch. Nearby was the general store pictured here, run by Arah's mother, Mary Sprague.

In 1917, John Holzwarth homesteaded land eight miles north of Grand Lake and also secured a second parcel of land. By the summer of 1918, the Holzwarths had collected a few cattle and built a cabin and barn on their first claim. When John was injured in a wagon accident and could no longer farm, the Holzwarth Ranch became the Holzwarth Trout Lodge. This picture shows the family in 1920.

The Holzwarth lodge rooms were rustic, but in the kitchen of their first cabin, called Mama Cabin, Sophia "Mama" Holzwarth prepared remarkable meals for the guests. She served trout, deer, grouse, and ranch-produced chicken, eggs, and milk. Travelers came by wagon and by Model T and Model A automobiles. Over the years, the Holzwarths added more cabins.

Tourist trade increased, and in 1929, the Holzwarths developed another guest ranch, the Never Summer Ranch, on their nearby property. Other buildings were constructed over the years. This 1973 photograph taken by Dwight L. Hamilton, park naturalist, shows John Holzwarth's son, Johnnie, riding with the Never Summer Mountains in the background.

This picture of the Holzwarth Ranch in snow was taken by Dwight L. Hamilton, park naturalist, in 1974. John Holzwarth Sr. died in 1932, and at that time, Mama Holzwarth stopped providing her home-cooked meals to tourists. The Trout Lodge quarters became housekeeping cabins where guests cooked their own meals on wood-burning stoves.

William Workman, a Kansas doctor, moved his practice to Denver in 1902. Soon after arriving, he bought land in Moraine Park from Abner Sprague for a summer home. He hiked, explored, and named many features in the area, including Fern Lake. About 1910, he built a fishing lodge on the shore of Fern Lake near the outlet.

In 1910, Dr. Workman sold the Fern Lake fishing lodge to the Higby brothers, who in turn sold it to others. At first, this was a summer camp with guests housed in tents. Beginning in 1917, it often hosted outings by the Colorado Mountain Club, and the storehouse became a dormitory. Later cabins and a dining room were added. This photograph shows the lodge in 1911.

William Allen White, editor and publisher of the *Emporia Gazette* in Emporia, Kansas, first came to the Big Thompson River in Moraine Park in the late 1880s, and he honeymooned there in 1893. The couple often came in summers to the Colorado Springs area, and in June 1911, they rented a cabin in Estes Park where White wrote his second novel, *In the Heart of a Fool.*

In 1912, William Allen White purchased a cabin at the eastern end of Moraine Park. The Whites added a bathroom and 14-foot porch and then two small "bedroom" cabins and a study. The Whites and their friends and relatives began spending their summers here. Many of the visitors were university professors or political leaders.

The cabin remained in the White family until 1972, when White's son, William Lindsay White, sold the house and its contents to the National Park Service. This picture of the William Allen White home was taken by Robert J. Haines, park naturalist, in 1976. The cabin today is used to house summer visitors as part of the park's Artist in Residence Program.

Three

EARLY COMMERCIAL ACTIVITIES

Before it became a park in 1915, the Rocky Mountain National Park area was home to a number of varied commercial activities. No one knows exactly how many people poured into the Estes Park area in the 1870s and 1880s, but more and more arrived each year. Adventurous travelers loved what they found and wrote about what they saw, which encouraged others to venture into Colorado. Some extolled the magnificent scenery. Others wrote about the fabulous hunting and fishing. To accommodate visitors, many of the early settlers opened and operated popular guest facilities.

In addition to successful tourist businesses, hunting, ranching, mining, and lumbering also prospered. Some of the earliest visitors to the park area, such as the Earl of Dunraven, were lured by the possibilities of hunting. In fact, the earl eyed the land for a private hunting preserve. Others saw hunting not just as a sport, but as an economic enterprise, selling the meat of game animals for profit. The earl and many others who caught their first glimpse of the Rocky Mountain Park area saw its potential to support dairying and cattle ranching. In the Kawuneechee Valley on the western slope, prospectors came in search of gold and silver. Large veins of ore had been found elsewhere in the Rockies. Why not here? As more and more prospectors came, mining towns grew up. Some boomed and busted within two or three years, changing from bustling camps to ghost towns. Others lasted. In either case, lumbering and sawmills were needed to build the homes and stores. All of these commercial activities were carried out from the 1870s until the time the land was set aside as a park in 1915.

The Earl of Dunraven, linked to English nobility, was enormously wealthy. Although he failed in his original plan to purchase all of the Estes Park area for a private hunting preserve, he did succeed in building and running a hunting lodge, a hotel, and a ranch, and in introducing Swiss cattle. This photograph shows a herd of cows at what was locally called "The English Dairy."

Although probably most of the people who came to Colorado during the Pike's Peak gold rush came to seek gold, many came for other reasons, or at least turned to other occupations when mining proved too much work for too little gain. Some settlers ran stores to meet the needs of miners. Other ran sawmills. The Dan Griffith Sawmill pictured here, which operated at Bierstadt Lake in 1907, is typical.

Small settlements in the Rockies sprang into existence overnight. There was a frenzy of building as farmers, ranchers, and storekeepers poured in. To meet the needs of new residents, many sawmills ran all winter long. Where needed, lumber was even taken from the mills to building work sites by sleds. This picture shows the Griffith Sawmill near Bierstadt Lake during the winter of 1910.

Historians estimate that supporting the mining frontier required five times the number of people actually working in the mines. Ranchers supplied chicken, meat, and dairy products, which were sold in stores that required shopkeepers. Once houses were built, women came to live in the frontier towns. In this picture, some ladies make a day's outing of visiting the Griffith Sawmill at Bierstadt Lake in 1910.

Lumber was needed for building homes and stores, for use in mines, and for railroads that were extending into the major mining areas. Crews of men worked to fell huge trees, wrestle them on to horse-drawn wagons, and haul them to lumber mills. Here a crew of men is hauling logs at Hollowell Park.

The earliest cabins and houses built by settlers used logs with foundations of stone or dirt. These small logs were untrimmed. The next step up was to use logs flattened on two sides with joints and notches cut to the builder's preference. Larger buildings could be erected when sawmills were in operation. This 1900 photograph shows the sawmill crew at Hidden Valley.

Many of the Rocky Mountain National Park area's early and successful pioneers added sawmills to the list of operations in which they were involved. Alexander MacGregor operated a sawmill off and on until the time of his death in 1896. Abner Sprague ran the sawmill that is pictured in this 1895 photograph.

The lure of rich lodes of silver drew prospectors into the area near Grand Lake in the 1870s and 1880s. Grand Lake became a distribution point for such new mining towns as Lulu City, Gaskill, and Teller. Mining tents and new cabins sprang up throughout the mountains. This is a picture of the Ezra Kauffman mining camp in Lulu City in 1882.

Gold and silver strikes drew men like Joe Shipler to come prospecting. In 1879, Shipler staked two promising silver claims on the slopes of Shipler Mountain. He settled along the Grand (Colorado) River near his claims and built several log cabins and developed his mine. This picture of the Shipler cabins on the Lulu City Trail was taken by ranger H. Raymond Gregg in 1938.

There were plans for Lulu City, located in front of Thunder Mountain, to grow to 100 blocks, each with 16 lots, but this grand dream was never realized. Although over 40 houses went up, as well as a hotel, and miners were busy everywhere, the mining companies found they could not make a profit on low-yielding ore. Miners deserted their claims, and by December 1883, the boom had ended.

50

During the Colorado mining boom, there were some men who could see that there were ways to make money other than mining. Big profits came from real estate speculations and promoting the building of new towns. Two such promoters from Fort Collins were William B. Baker and Benjamin Franklin Burnett. There appeared to be rich lodes of silver in the area. Why not cash in by building a boom town? These two men formed the Middle Park and Grand River Mining Company to create Lulu City. By 1880, Burnett had a 160-acre town site, which he named for his daughter Lulu, who was reported to have been a great beauty in her youth. One resident of the area described Lulu as "the most beautiful girl I ever saw." This is a photograph of Lulu Burnett taken many years after Lulu City, which bore her name, had become a ghost town.

Here are the remains of a cabin in Lulu City. During its short heyday, Lulu City bustled. In addition to the mines, two sawmills ran day and night constructing cabins and stores. By 1881, there was a barbershop, a butcher shop, a clothing store, several grocery and liquor stores, and a dairy offering butter and milk. By 1886, Lulu City and all the other nearby mining towns were abandoned.

Brawling miners, no longer welcome in Lulu City, went only a short ways off and organized another mining camp called Dutchtown at timberline on the sides of Lead and Cirrus Mountains. Dutchtown lasted only slightly longer than Lulu City, and miners vacated their cabins in 1884. These remains of an abandoned Dutchtown cabin were photographed by ranger D. Ferrel Atkins in 1964.

This photograph shows the Eugenia Mine sign. The Eugenia Mine was located at 9,908 feet about six mines north of what is now Allenspark, Colorado. This mine was worked by Carl Norwall and his family. Norwall dug more than 1,000 feet into Battle Mountain trying to make his fortune but was rewarded with no ore of any value.

Carl Norwall built a fine cabin for his wife and two daughters, complete with a piano, only a few hundred feet downstream from his mine. Visitors today to Rocky Mountain National Park can take a 1.4-mile hike from the Longs Peak Ranger Station to the ruins of the cabin and mining machinery at the Eugenia Mine site.

This is the mining cabin of eccentric William Clyde Currance, known as "Miner Bill." Wild tales abound about this man who came to Estes Park in 1883. Because of his bizarre behavior, he spent time in the Colorado State Insane Asylum. On release, he filed two mining claims on the west side of Mount Chapin and built an elaborate trail to his mine and two cabins.

In 1962, park superintendent Roger Contor photographed someone looking into the Bill Currance Mine shaft. Miner Bill fought with the government during the building of the Fall River Road between 1913 and 1921. He finally went to live in Estes Park, where F. O. Stanley gave him odd jobs. After he was missing from town for a week, a searcher found Miner Bill dead outside his cabin.

Early pioneers in the Rocky Mountain National Park area made money by selling dressed game and skins in Denver. The earliest pioneers, Joel Estes and his family, went into Denver every two months to sell deer, elk, mountain sheep, and antelope. This bear hunting picture shows James Howard and Mr. and Mrs. Kline with their bear. Mr. Kline, with moustache, is on the right.

Sometimes troublesome animals are trapped and moved. Ranger Jack Moomaw trapped a 300-pound black bear that had rummaged around his cabin in the summer of 1932. The bear was taken to Chapin Pass and released. This is a picture of a bear trap near Lulu City in 1947.

Note the large-caliber rifle being held by buckskin-clad Mr. Harmon as he stands in front of his hunting shelter. Hunters in the late 1800s and early 1900s, meeting the demand of settlers and prospectors for meat, reduced the herds of bighorn sheep and elk from their early levels of thousands of animals to only a few hundred by 1912.

In the early years after the establishment of Rocky Mountain National Park, many of its rules regarding park wildlife were not clearly refined. In some cases, hunters were paid to eliminate predatory animals like mountain lions so that elk and deer would be protected and thrive. This 1922 photograph shows John Griffith with a mountain lion.

Four

FORMATION AND GROWTH OF ROCKY MOUNTAIN NATIONAL PARK

In 1907 and 1908, various regional plans were being discussed to address such topics as wildlife protection in the magnificent mountainous area that is now Rocky Mountain National Park. Some proposed the area be turned into a game refuge. But others, led by Enos Mills, thought in much larger terms. They wanted far more protection than a game park provided or than was available by designation as a national forest. Mills and other like-minded conservationists wanted to establish a national park. Mills's original plan for such a park called for 1,000 square miles of land with Estes Park in the center. Such a plan led to vehement opposition by many groups and individuals, including H. N. Wheeler of the forest service.

Mills continued his efforts to create a park. Thanks to compromise bills reducing the area of land, which were drawn up by James Grafton Rogers and which made the park plan more palatable, Congress finally passed a bill creating the park that was signed by Pres. Woodrow Wilson in 1915. Creation of luxury spots like the Stanley Hotel brought many new visitors. This number greatly increased with the improvement of local roads and the construction of Trail Ridge Road through the park.

The number of park facilities and personnel expanded yearly to meet the needs of a growing public. In 1929, the Never Summer Range was added to the park. Today Rocky Mountain National Park hosts more than three million visitors a year. It is accessible by three roads, encompasses 265,770 acres, contains five drive-in campgrounds and 369 miles of trails, and has over 60 named peaks that are higher than 12,000 feet. The mission of the park service is to "preserve this natural treasure unimpaired for the enjoyment of this and future generations."

James Grafton Rogers, a Denver attorney, assisted Enos Mills when opposition arose over the formation of a park. Mills envisioned a "Mountain Climbing Organization" whose objective was to create Rocky Mountain National Park. The Colorado Mountain Club resulted from this effort and held its first meeting in April 1912. Rogers went on to draft park bills sent to Congress over the next three years.

Since Enos Mills's original proposal was opposed by local and mining interests, changes were necessary if a park bill was to make it through Congress. James Grafton Rogers drafted compromise legislation that angered Mills. The new bill finally passed Congress and was signed by Pres. Woodrow Wilson on January 26, 1915. The formal dedication ceremony, commemorated by this seal, was held on September 4, 1915, at Horseshoe Park.

As Enos Mills opened the ceremonies to dedicate the newly formed Rocky Mountain National Park, rain began to fall, but rain could not dampen the enthusiasm generated by the event, which was proclaimed by proud banners. An estimated 2,000 people attended the dedication. Many came on foot, on horseback, and in carriages. As the ceremonies continued, the rain stopped, clouds parted, the sun shone, and Longs Peak came into view.

Nearby cities announced the time and place of the dedication ceremonies in their newspapers and fanned a friendly rivalry among cities by encouraging people who drove to Horseshoe Park to display the names of their communities on banners affixed to their automobiles. Some said it was the largest gathering of automobiles yet in the state of Colorado.

Many distinguished guests attended the colorful park dedication ceremonies held in 1915, including Stephen Mather, associate Secretary of the Interior, who was soon to become the first director of the National Park Service. With Mather in this picture are Gov. George Carlson, Abner Sprague, and representatives of the Este's Park Women's Club.

Among those pictured here at the Rocky Mountain National Park dedication ceremony are Enos Mills (no hat), who had campaigned so long and hard for this park. Standing immediately to the left of Mills and holding a small flag is F. O. Stanley, a staunch supporter of the park who was a wealthy inventor and the owner of the Stanley Hotel in Estes Park.

For health reasons, Freelan Oscar Stanley moved to Estes Park, where he and his wife, Flora, lived in a rented cabin. In 1906, they built a home on Wonder View Avenue. Stanley purchased 1,400 acres of land from the Earl of Dunraven and began planning a luxury hotel. Believing that magnificent scenery would attract guests from the East Coast, Stanley began work on the hotel, which was completed in 1909.

Freelan Oscar Stanley and his twin brother, Francis, are shown in this 1917 photograph driving one of their famous Stanley Steamer automobiles. The brothers made their fortune first by developing and selling a successful dry-plate photography business, and then by designing an early car with a steam engine. After selling their original design, they designed a new and improved car marketed under the name Stanley Steamer.

Guests came to the Stanley Hotel from Denver in a fleet of Stanley Steamer automobiles. Over the next 10 years, Stanley kept busy with many projects to improve the town of Estes Park. He built a hydroelectric plant, gave land for a fairgrounds and city park, and improved roads. Carriages and Stanley Steamer automobiles comingle in this 1912 photograph taken in Estes Park.

The Stanley Hotel boasted a first-class kitchen, an elegant billiard room, and a music room that featured of view of Longs Peak out the window. There were tennis courts and an 18-hole golf course. A horseback party takes advantage of the extensive grounds at the Stanley Hotel in this picture taken by George A. Grant in 1938.

This 1965 photograph taken by park ranger Pat Miller shows the construction of the new park headquarters and visitor center at Beaver Meadows. In addition to this headquarters complex, the park also contains the Kawuneechee Visitor Center, the Alpine Visitor Center, the Lily Lake Visitor Center, and the Moraine Park Museum. In addition, there are information kiosks and seasonal information stations.

This 1967 photograph taken by naturalist Wayne B. Alcorn shows the completed headquarters building and Beaver Meadows Visitor Center. Designed by the Frank Lloyd Wright School of Architecture at Taliesin West in Scottsdale, Arizona, it is a National Historical Landmark. In the background is majestic Longs Peak, the highest mountain in the park standing at 14,259 feet.

The dedication ceremony for the new Rocky Mountain National Park Headquarters at Beaver Meadows took place on June 24, 1967, and was captured in this photograph by park naturalist Wayne B. Alcorn. The design for this building incorporated the park's popular rustic style, integrating the buildings into their natural setting. The surrounding utility buildings are examples of the rustic-style buildings that the Civilian Conservation Corps built during the Depression. Rocky Mountain National Park has grown from its 1915 beginnings with the additional land of the Never Summer Range and through building and improving roads and facilities like the new park headquarters. In 1914, an estimated 56,000 people visited the region. By 2002, there were 3.3 million visitors, and this number grows each year. Expansion of park services continues today as the park looks forward to its 100th anniversary in 2015.

Five

OUTDOOR FUN IN THE PARK

Some who visit the park are content to look and admire the great natural beauty of the outdoors found here in abundance. Others want to capture it in some way and take it away with them. Rocky Mountain National Park is an artists' delight. Some sketch, some paint, and others photograph the wildlife, massive peaks, alpine meadows, tumbling streams, placid lakes, and gushing waterfalls. Around every curve of Trail Ridge Road is another sight to make viewers catch their breath.

Many visitors want to do more than see and catch the beauty of the scene. They want to participate in summer activities such as hiking, bird watching, identifying wildflowers, rock climbing, camping, and fishing. There are hundreds of drive-in campsites in the park where campers can park trailers or pitch tents. Many backcountry sites are available for those who are well equipped and able to hike into wilderness areas. Anglers test their skills against four kinds of trout found in the park's lakes and streams. Although most park visitors come in summer, the park is open in winter, too. Then for fun, visitors turn to snow-related activities, including skiing, snowshoeing, and ice climbing

It seems that no one who comes to the park to spend time in the outdoors and unspoiled wilderness leaves disappointed. There is enough variety and activity for all. Naturalist Enos Mills, who played a major role in founding Rocky Mountain National Park, anticipated the joy and fun that visitors to the region would appreciate for generations to come. He wrote, "This is a beautiful world, and all who go out under the open sky will feel the gentle, kindly influence of nature and hear her good tidings."

This 1888 photograph taken by F. E. Chapin shows his campsite near Ypsilon Creek. The creek flows out of Ypsilon Lake and joins Roaring Fork. Chapin's wife named Ypsilon Mountain, and another peak in the Mummy Range was later named for Chapin. One of the early explorers in the range, Chapin wrote extensively about his experiences and in 1889 published his book, *Mountaineering in Colorado.*

A group of campers set up their tent, table, and fireplace in 1908 at Bierstadt Lake. Several features in the park are named for noted artist Albert Bierstadt, who first came to the Estes Park area in the fall of 1876 as the guest of the Earl of Dunraven. He painted and sketched scenes of the area and helped select the site for the building of the English Hotel.

This early camping scene shows a group of men and women enjoying an outing in the Rocky Mountain National Park area. Campers are able to enjoy forests of spruce and fir, and when they walk at lower elevations, they find aspen and willows lining the meandering streams. In late summer and early fall, wildflowers add to the beauty of the meadows.

Here a camper demonstrates his skill at flipping flapjacks. Those who fill their days with strenuous outdoor activities like to begin their morning with a hearty breakfast. The lucky fishermen among them may find themselves enjoying a dinner of fresh-caught trout come evening campfire, while those less successful may have to content themselves with store-bought food.

Only five years after the land was set aside as a national park, this young couple set up their campsite on the shore of Bear Lake in 1920. Nestled in a glacial valley at 9,500 feet, Bear Lake serves as a hub for many park activities. It is a trailhead for hikes and snow trips to Dream, Bierstadt, and Odessa Lakes and to Flattop Mountain.

In 1925, a group of campers set a boat in the waters of Bear Lake. Today, although kayaks and canoes are permitted in many of the lakes in Rocky Mountain National Park, they are not permitted in Bear Lake. The lake rests just beneath the flanks of Hallett Peak and the Continental Divide and provides an excellent view of Longs Peak.

This old automobile supports part of the tent cover around 1927 when a camper from Texas takes time to care for her long hair. The early success of Rocky Mountain National Park as a tourist attraction was dependent on the automobile, which brought out-of-staters to the Estes Park area. Way back in 1912, Colorado's governor John F. Shafroth said good roads would make Colorado "a playground for the world."

Al Rozum, ranger at Rocky Mountain National Park, photographed these hikers on the trail above Dream Lake pausing to look at Tyndall Gorge and Hallett Peak during the summer of 1954. Dream Lake occupies a glaciated U-shaped valley. At the head of the gorge between Hallett Peak and Flattop Mountain is Tyndall Glacier, one of the few glaciers in the park.

Even in summertime, visitors to the park may find themselves walking on snow, as did these visitors to Chasm Lake in July 1986. Chasm Lake is an alpine lake at 11,760 feet of elevation that lies at the base of the east face of Longs Peak. The cirque, or amphitheater, in which Chasm Lake is located was left behind by a mountain glacier.

A group of hikers on the Dream Lake trail looking toward Longs Peak are seen in this August 1954 photograph taken by park ranger Al Rozum. They have stopped to rest and to catch a view of Glacier Gorge and the north side of Longs Peak. From Dream Lake, the trail continues on to either Emerald Lake or Lake Haiyaha.

Several small glaciers and permanent snowfields are found in the park in the high mountain cirques. These include Andrews Glacier, Sprague Glacier, Taylor Glacier, Rowe Glacier, Mills Glacier, Moomaw Glacier, and Tyndall Glacier (pictured here). In 1900, these five visitors try their luck at ascending Tyndall Glacier. Ice axes and a rope help keep the group together and prevent slipping on the slope.

Nearly one-third of Rocky Mountain National Park is above tree line, which is at 11,400 feet of elevation. One of the biggest challenges to climbers is Longs Peak. Thousands of visitors attempt the ascent each year, most using the popular Keyhole route. In this July 1924 photograph, Ed Stopher is at a section of the trail known as "The Trough."

AGNES VAILLE DIES IN STORM AFTER CLIMBING LONGS PEAK

Body of Chamber of Commerce Secretary Found Frozen in Snow.

(Continued From Page One.)

Oscar Brown; Jacob Christy and Herbert Sortland, all employed at the inn. Sortland became exhausted after going about a mile from the house and, suffering from a frozen face and frozen ears, left the party and started back to the shelter. That was the last any of the party saw of the man and it is feared that he fell exhausted in the deep snow and froze to death. Thermometers carried by Kiener showed a temperature of 50 degrees below zero. The heavy snow storm, virtually a blizzard, which raged on the peak yesterday, was accompanied by a strong wind.

Body Found Frozen in Snow.

When the party of men reached the spot where Kiener had left his companion, they found her lying in the snow, dead from the cold and exposure. She had evidently succumbed to her desire for sleep, natural to one slowly freezing to death, and had died but a short time before her rescuers reached her. She had been alone on the mountain saddle from 11 o'clock yesterday morning to 4 o'clock yesterday afternoon, when the men found her body. Kiener's journey to the shelter house and the return trip of the party consuming this amount of time because of the severity of the storm.

... be brought down ...

AGNES W. VAILLE.

Late in 1924, Agnes Vaille and Walter Kiener attempted the first winter ascent of the east face of Longs Peak. After reaching the top, Vaille was exhausted. She fell coming down and could not continue. Kiener went for help but Vaille had frozen to death before he returned. This newspaper clipping from the Rocky Mountain News provides a photograph of Agnes Vaille and an account of her death.

A plaque at the Keyhole at the Agnes Vaille Memorial Shelter commemorates Vaille's climb of Longs Peak and her death on January 12, 1925, as well as the death of Herbert Sortland, who lost his life as one of the members of the rescue crew who tried unsuccessfully to reach her and bring her back to safety. Rescue attempts were hindered by low temperatures, deep snow, and wind.

Agnes Vaille was not the first woman to die climbing Longs Peak. Carrie Welton climbed to the summit in 1884. She became exhausted on her climb down and sent her guide for help. On the guide's return, he found Carrie Welton dead from exposure. Recognizing the dangers associated with climbing the peak, the park service built a shelter at the Longs Peak boulder field in 1927. In 1935, another, smaller stone shelter was built by Vaille's family in her memory. Park ranger Curtis Skinner photographed the Agnes Wolcott Vaille memorial shelter at the Keyhole on July 23, 1937. The dangers associated with climbing the peak did not discourage enthusiasts. In fact, in the year 1929 alone, only four years after the death of Agnes Vaille, 1,600 people signed the register at the top of Longs Peak.

In the late 1920s, other routes were explored up Longs Peak. Documented in this 1927 photograph is the first ascent of Stettner's Ledges on the east face of Long Peak. Paul and Joe Stettner from Chicago explored this route. They had learned climbing in the German and Austrian Alps before immigrating to the United States. The Stettners' route was perhaps the most difficult climb in the country at that time.

In August 1925, ranger Moomaw and two workmen installed a steel cable on the north side of Longs Peak. The galvanized cable had been manufactured to sustain a load of five tons. The cable was fastened by strong pins firmly imbedded in granite. Wearing a hat and a striking hiking costume, this woman holds the cable to assist her in a 1927 photograph taken by park superintendent Roger W. Toll.

The top of Ouzel Peak is broad and flat with the highest point on the eastern edge. Dressed in knickers and a cap, this woman stands triumphant at the Ouzel Peak summit. Park ranger Curtis Skinner caught the proud moment in this 1927 photograph. Some skilled people return from the climb in early summer by sliding down the snowfield situated on the northern flank of the peak.

Bear Lake is located in a beautiful part of the park at 9,300 feet of elevation. It supports many forms of recreation. There is an interpretive 0.6-mile nature hike circling the lake with information on glaciation and sub-alpine life. This rock climber practices climbing above Bear Lake. Park ranger Jerry Phillips snapped this picture on June 28, 1959.

Eagle Cliff Mountain at 8,906 feet in elevation is one of the lower elevation cliffs that lie along the eastern edge of Rocky Mountain National Park. On an August day in 1963, this dapper climber with pipe is photographed during his climb. Also attracted to the craggy rock outcroppings are such birds as golden eagles, peregrine and prairie falcons, kestrels, red-tailed and Cooper hawks, and turkey vultures.

Abner Sprague, one of the earliest settlers in the Rocky Mountain National Park area, is the highest person in this picture with his climbing party atop Longs Peak in 1924. The first recorded ascent of Longs Peak took place in August 1868. That small climbing group was led by John Wesley Powell and included William Byers, the founder of Denver's first newspaper, the *Rocky Mountain News*.

The string of fish proudly displayed in this photograph documents the success of a group of anglers at Bear Lake. This lake is no longer open to fishing. Within the park, there are open lakes where fishing is permitted, closed waters, and catch-and-release areas where only barbless hooks are permitted. A Colorado fishing license is required, and visitors must abide by park regulations and restrictions.

Fishing was popular with early settlers in the area. To improve the sport, the park stocked many streams with nonnative species of trout. Since 1975, nonnative fish have been removed from some waters, while native Greenback cutthroat and Colorado River cutthroat trout have been restored. Today's lucky fisherman may find brown, brook, rainbow, and cutthroat trout. This 1930 picture shows an angler at Bear Lake.

The Estes Park Fish Hatchery opened in 1907 with the aim of promoting tourism. It was a community effort taken on by the Estes Park Protective and Improvement Association. The land located next to Fall River was a gift from rancher Pieter Hondius. This photograph of the hatchery was taken by John C. Preston in 1932.

Women admire the successful Estes Park Fish Hatchery. It was managed by Gaylord Thomson, who kept a pet fish there named Sunbeam. In 1909, four sizing ponds were added. The State of Colorado made some major renovations in 1928 and 1929 when they managed the facility. The hatchery operated until 1982, when it was put out of commission by the Lawn Lake flood.

This fisherman holds a German brown caught on July 15, 1959. Weighing 13 pounds 8 ounces, this fish was pulled from Lake Granby. Originally a European game fish, it was introduced into Rocky Mountain National Park where it lives in lakes and streams. The German brown is light brown to tawny black, becoming silvery on the sides and belly. It grows faster and lives longer than other varieties of trout.

Beaver are semi-aquatic rodents that sometimes dam streams in shallow valleys, creating ponds and wetlands. They may build a lodge in the middle of a pond with an underwater entrance. This protects beaver from enemies, such as coyotes, and also provides access to winter food. In this 1938 picture, a woman is fishing in a Hidden Valley beaver pond known for its brook trout.

This fisherman tests his luck on the east shore of Bear Lake in July 1955. Although there are restrictions with respect to size and limit of fish, as well as designated "catch and release" areas, fishing is still permitted in most lakes and streams in Rocky Mountain National Park. This is not the case at Bear Lake, where fishing is no longer allowed.

Park naturalist Robert J. Haines took this picture at Bear Lake of two ice fisherman in December 1973. Like fly-fishing, ice fishing in Rocky Mountain National Park requires a Colorado state fishing license. Those who attempt it may need to snowshoe or ski to reach ice fishing sites. At Grand Lake, the western gateway to the park, ice fishing derbies are held in January and February.

Nordic, or cross-country skiing, is a popular winter sport in Rocky Mountain National Park. Experienced skiers explore a stunning winter landscape. Moderate to deep snow covers high valleys between December and May. This photograph by Thomas J. Allen, who later became park superintendent, was taken along the Fall River Road in March 1923.

Park ranger C. E. Humberger took this winter ski picture in 1942 that shows Hallett Peak from the Bear Lake area. As it is for summer activities, Bear Lake is a central departure point for many winter trips. Rocky Mountain National Park's glacially carved terrain lends itself to ski touring and ski mountaineering.

A cross-country skier is caught in this photograph taken by Supt. Roger Contor in January 1959. Generally ski touring takes place in the lower valleys, especially in the Bear Lake and Wild Basin areas. In other parts of the park, experienced athletes enjoy ski mountaineering that involves steep climbs and descents, narrow routes, and sharp turns.

The Hidden Valley ski area of Estes Park officially opened in 1955, but long before lifts were installed, local residents used this spot for downhill skiing. This jumper at Hidden Valley was photographed by park naturalist Robert J. Haines in April 1965. Originally the area was run by the Estes Park Recreation District and backed by local businesses.

In March 1956, park management assistant Gordon Patterson took this picture of downhill skiers at Hidden Valley. The area was bought by the park service with the intent to phase out the ski operation. The double chair lift was removed in 1977. In 1991, the ski area was closed and re-vegetation carried out. Today it is enjoyed by tubers and sledders.

In this picture taken in 1920, a horse struggles through deep snow on the top of Flattop Mountain. During summer outings, many visitors in the park use horses. When people are on horseback, many wild animals such as elk do not seem to notice them, so horseback riding in Rocky Mountain National Park provides some great opportunities for watching wildlife.

This photograph of riders on the Flattop Mountain trail was snapped by park superintendent Roger Contor in July 1958. Bear Lake is the start of this switchback trail that affords a glimpse directly down at Dream Lake and Emerald Lake. Looking across the way to the south provides a view of Glacier Gorge. In Glacier Gorge, one can see Mills Lake, and at the head of the gorge is majestic Longs Peak. Looking east, one gets views of Bear Lake, Sprague Lake, and Bierstadt Lake. Many trails in Rocky Mountain National Park are open to horses and other pack animals, including mules, burros, and llamas. There are regulations, including having no more than 20 animals in a string. Horses and guides are available inside the park and also from a number of liveries outside the east and west boundaries of the park.

Six

MAJOR CONSTRUCTION PROJECTS

Although many people in the late 1800s looked at the beautiful land in the Estes Park area and thought of preservation, others thought mainly about its use. With the completion of a railroad from Denver to Cheyenne, eastern slope farmers saw new markets and eyed meltwater for irrigation. Gradually an idea developed to divert water from what is now the northwest corner of Rocky Mountain National Park to the eastern plains through La Poudre Pass and down the Cache La Poudre River. The Larimer County Ditch Company started construction of the Grand Ditch along the Never Summer Range. Each summer, it grew longer, and three miles were completed in 1894. After the formation of the park, Congress approved taking park land for the Long Draw Reservoir. Another act of Congress approved lengthening the ditch three miles, and the Grand Ditch project was finally completed in 1936.

The Grand Ditch was not the only project facing those concerned with preservation of the new park's land. Almost immediately, everyone realized better roads were necessary. The Fall River Road across the Continental Divide that was built between 1913 and 1920 was not adequate to handle the traffic coming into the new national park. In 1929, construction began on Trail Ridge Road, which was completed in 1932. Great pains were taken to protect the environment as this road was built.

Additional construction took place in Rocky Mountain National Park during the Great Depression, when small groups of the Civilian Conservation Corps were housed in the park. They worked on park buildings and improved trails and overlooks.

To secure additional water for the semiarid eastern plains, Colorado farmers proposed building a tunnel under Otis Peak through Rocky Mountain National Park to provide irrigation water and hydroelectric power. Although many groups opposed it, on December 21, 1937, Pres. Franklin Roosevelt approved funding to begin the Colorado Big Thompson Project. On June 23, 1947, the first water flowed through the Alva B. Adams Tunnel from Grand Lake to Lake Estes and down the Big Thompson River. Additional tunnels, power stations, dams, and reservoirs were completed by 1954.

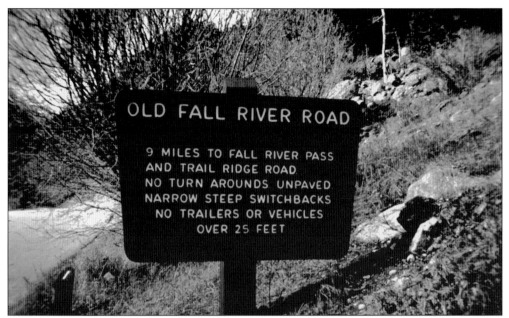

Building a useable road across the Continental Divide had been discussed for a number of years. It was not until 1913 that the State of Colorado agreed to fund the project. The road would connect Estes Park and Grand Lake with a scenic route across the Divide. This road sign reminds tourists about to turn onto the road that it is steep, narrow, and offers no place to turn around.

In September 1913, convicts from the Colorado State Penitentiary moved into cabins along the Fall River. They served as the work crew for the seven-year Fall River Road construction project. Businessmen and Rocky Mountain Park enthusiasts alike realized that more and more people would be coming to tour the area. After early work, traditional road crews replaced the convicts.

Keeping the Fall River Road clear of snow was always a problem. In 1913, after construction on the road began in September, the severest snowstorm in the state's history hit during the first five days of December and halted construction. Four feet of snow covered the ground. Once the road was finished, steam shovels, like this one photographed in 1925, had the difficult job of clearing the snow.

In 1921, park superintendent L. C. Way stands beside the automobile that was the first car on Fall River Road. In addition to automobiles, Circle Tours became popular. Tourists would get on a bus in Denver, drive to Estes Park for an overnight, then go to Grand Lake via the Fall River Road, and back to Denver over Berthoud Pass.

These early visitors on the Fall River Road leave their car to take in some of the remarkable scenery in the area. Among the many points of interest for 1920s tourists was a stop at Chasm Falls where tourists could cross a bridge and watch the falls below. The bridge was removed following an accident.

When completed, the Fall River Road left Endovalley and climbed by way of 16 switchbacks a distance of 9.4 miles to Fall River Pass. Driving the road was a challenge to ordinary motorists and to the Rocky Mountain Park Company buses. By 1937, automobile traffic on Fall River Road was more common. These people are parked at the Fall River Pass store.

Some cars could not negotiate the road. Some navigated the switchbacks in reverse because their reverse gears had more power than their low one. Even though there were difficulties in traveling over Fall River Road, it was popular. Tourists in snow caravans like the one pictured here had an exciting and exhilarating experience.

Park superintendent Roger Toll took this picture in October 1922 of a bridge over Alpine Brook on the Longs Peak Road. This small side road leading from the main road between Estes Park and Allenspark (currently known as the Peak to Peak Highway) gave automobile access to the east trailhead of Longs Peak.

The old Fall River Road was hard to keep free of snow and difficult to drive at best, so by the middle of the 1920s, there was uniform agreement that a new road was desperately needed. Construction began in 1929 on Trail Ridge Road and was completed in 1932. The highest point on this road is at an elevation of 12,183 feet.

Congress approved $450,000 for the construction of Trail Ridge Road in April 1929. The contract for building the eastern portion of the highway went to W. A. Colt of Las Animas. Colt knew that most work would have to be done between the snow-free periods of mid-June to mid-October. Pictured here is early construction on Trail Ridge Road in 1929.

Hidden Valley was a base camp for some of the Trail Ridge Road construction crew. Colt had 150 laborers to work on the eastern portion, along with 35 men who served in such jobs as foremen, mechanics, power-shovel operators, and cooks. This 1929 picture gives a good view of the rough and rocky terrain where the men worked.

The contract for the western portion of Trail Ridge Road from Fall River Pass to the floor of the Colorado River Valley went to L. T. Lawler of Butte, Montana. In August 1930, this surveyor is at work. Although progress was rapid in the summer, it stopped with early snows. The severe winter of 1930–1931 held up the western construction crew until May and the eastern crew until June.

In this picture, a construction crew labors on Trail Ridge Road, trying to complete as soon as possible a scenic highway into the area. The need for a modern highway was clear. Rocky Mountain National Park was well established by 1929. That year, nearly 300,000 people entered the park. It had become a booming recreational area.

Road crews tried to lessen environmental damage. After a blast, debris was removed and displaced rocks were put back in place, lichen-side up. In addition to foremen, park officials traveled up and down the road to see that work was being done properly. Chief ranger John McLaughlin took this photograph in August 1932 of rock-cut construction work on Trail Ridge Road.

In 1933, Trail Ridge Road, called "Highway to the Sky," was opened, although paving work continued for several years. On its completion, the *Rocky Mountain News* called this highway the "scenic wonder of the world." About 10 miles of the road were above 11,000 feet. No grade was steeper than seven percent.

The first unemployed men who constituted the beginning of the Colorado group of the Civilian Conservation Corps (CCC) arrived in Rocky Mountain National Park on May 12, 1933. This program provided men to work on such projects as improving trails, building overlooks, and chopping down beetle-killed trees. This is a photograph of the CCC Camp NP-11-C, No. 2, taken by ranger H. Raymond Gregg in February 1941.

The controversial Alva Adams Tunnel brought water to Colorado farmers on the semiarid eastern plain. The tunnel had been opposed by conservationists and urged forward by farmers with political clout. President Roosevelt approved a feasibility study in 1937 to begin what was called the Colorado–Big Thompson Project. This crowd of people photographed by ranger H. Raymond Gregg is at the east side of the Alva Adams Tunnel in 1940.

On June 23, 1947, the first water flowed eastward through the Alva Adams Tunnel from Grand Lake. The 13.1-mile aqueduct carried water under Otis Peak on the Continental Divide to Lake Estes. Water is delivered to cities and towns and helps irrigate thousands of acres of northeastern Colorado farmland. Naturalist Robert J. Haines took this picture of the east portal of the Alva Adams Tunnel on February 8, 1977.

Seven

DANGERS IN THE PARK

Any national park is subject to a variety of dangers to people, property, and the park land itself. Over the years, Rocky Mountain National Park has had its share of problems. Many disasters overlap, but the biggest dangers facing people are getting lost, being injured from a fall, inclement weather, being struck by lightning, or being attacked by a wild animal. Property is most often damaged when there is a destructive flood, while the greatest damage to park land is fire.

Rescue teams spring into action when a hiker is reported missing or a climber is in trouble. Typical was the 1956 rescue on Hallett Peak of Patrick Dwyer. Dwyer was attempting this difficult climb when he fell 200 feet and slid another 200 feet before coming to stop on a rocky ledge. The rangers who rescued him under very difficult and dangerous conditions were given the National Park Service Valor Award. Three people were struck by lightning very near the Alpine Visitor Center in July 1999, and one died. Patrick Finan and Tim Shuett survived a bear attack at their campsite in July 2003 near Fern Lake.

The main source of water in the Big Thompson Flood was the North Fork of the Big Thompson River, which originates in Rocky Mountain National Park. The flood in the summer of 1976 was the worst natural disaster to ever occur in Colorado. One hundred and forty-five people were killed, and the loss was listed at $40 million. The bursting of the Lawn Lake dam sent flood waters down the Roaring River in Rocky Mountain National Park in 1982. It caused three deaths, ripped through the Aspenglen Campground, wiped out a fish hatchery, and caused extensive damage in Estes Park.

Over the years, the park has seen many destructive wildfires, some caused by campers and others by lightning. Representative is the Ouzel Lake wildfire of 1978. Winds whipped flames into a blaze, threatening the small mountain community of Allenspark as well as park land. The fire burned 1,050 acres before it was extinguished.

Wildfires constituted a danger before and after the formation of Rocky Mountain National Park. This photograph shows trees at the edge of Bierstadt Lake wiped out by fire in 1900. Most wildfires in the park area are caused by lightning. Although fire is a natural part of the park ecosystem, fires are suppressed when they threaten people or widespread damage to portions of the park or surrounding communities.

When there have been no fires in an area for some time, fuel in the form of dead and diseased trees builds up. Then a fire can be potentially devastating. These are trees after the burn of 1900 at Bierstadt Lake. Because fires thin forests, recycle nutrients into the soil, and release seeds, carefully monitored prescribed burns are sometimes made in the park.

When the first smoke from the Ouzel Lake fire in Rocky Mountain National Park was discovered in the summer of 1978, a decision was made not to suppress it. This fire resulted from a lightning strike in what was designated a low-risk zone above 10,000 feet. The fire in a sub-alpine spruce and fir forest did little but smolder for the next 10 days, increasing in size very slowly.

On August 23, 1978, the Ouzel Lake fire, which was being carefully monitored, flared up and reached tree crowns. Ouzel and Bluebird Lakes and backcountry sites in the park were closed to hikers and campers. Over the next eight days, the fire crept forward into an area between Ouzel Lake and the Chickadee Pond. High winds developed on September 1, and crews began working to suppress the fire.

Twenty-eight firefighters began working from a base camp equipped with a tool cache that was set up on the trail outside the eastern perimeter. The crews worked to suppress the Ouzel Lake fire along its east side and in the northeast corner. A helicopter is pictured here dropping water on the Ouzel Lake fire.

This photograph shows an Ouzel Lake fire crew at work. By September 5, 1978, the fire seemed stable and firefighting crews were reduced. Snow and rain on September 11 further lessoned the fire danger. But on September 15, thirty mile-per-hour winds whipped the fire back into life and pushed it toward the park boundary. The park service requested help from the Boise Inter-Agency Fire Center.

On September 22, 1978, fifteen crews returned to the fire line. Fire crews worked in the Ouzel Lake fire using four portable pumps and 5,000 feet of hose. A second snowstorm began. On September 25, the fire was officially reported as contained. Mop-up work continued until September 30, when the fire was declared under control. The Ouzel Lake wildfire had burned 1050 acres.

The Twin Sisters Peaks are located on the eastern edge of Rocky Mountain National Park. A fire lookout building stood there on the main summit at an elevation of 11,412 feet. It overlooked the Tahosa Valley to the west. This photograph of the Twin Sisters fire lookout was taken in July 1937.

Robert Haines, park naturalist, took this photograph in July 1968 of a firefighter using an Osborn Fire Finder at the Twin Sisters Fire Lookout Station. The tower was once an active station in the area's fire management plan. The lookout tower was removed in 1977. There is now a radio antenna and relay station atop the peak.

Fire lookout Griffith is captured scanning for fires in this 1960 photograph taken by ranger Jerome Kasten at the Shadow Mountain lookout. The fire lookout near the summit of the mountain was one of four fire detection towers built during the Great Depression by members of the Civilian Conservation Corps. It was in active use from 1933 to 1968. The building has been restored by the Rocky Mountain Nature Association.

Lightning strikes are not unusual in Colorado. This picture of a lightning storm was taken from Trail Ridge Road. A rule of thumb for hikers in the high country of Rocky Mountain National Park is to be up high by noon and back down by 2:00 to avoid afternoon thunderstorms.

Colorado ranks in the top 10 states in annual lightning strike fatalities. On average, Colorado sees 3 fatalities and 14 injuries a year from lightning. Park rangers advise that it is safer for visitors to hike in the morning than in the afternoon. Ethel B. Ridenour was wearing these clothes when struck by lighting in Rocky Mountain National Park on September 1, 1923.

Storms come up quickly in Rocky Mountain National Park. Visitors and hikers are urged to use preventative measures and, when a storm kicks up, to head down off the mountain. Lightning strikes are most common from May to September. The clothes worn by Ethel D. Ridenour hanging on the line in this picture show the extent of damage from a lighting strike in 1923.

This tree in Horseshoe Park in Rocky Mountain National Park was struck by lightning. It is estimated that three to seven fires yearly are caused in the park by lightning strikes. Lightning has been known to strike 5 to 10 miles away from the thunderstorm, and a lightning strike can occur before, during, or after rain.

Avalanches are common in the high country of Colorado. This photograph taken on May 21, 1926, by park superintendent Thomas J. Allen shows avalanches on Mount Chapin taken from across the valley. Avalanche danger increases after a new snow or a heavy windstorm. Many winter sports enthusiasts take courses in avalanche awareness and safety. Some skiers carry electronic transceivers with them when they ski to facilitate rescue.

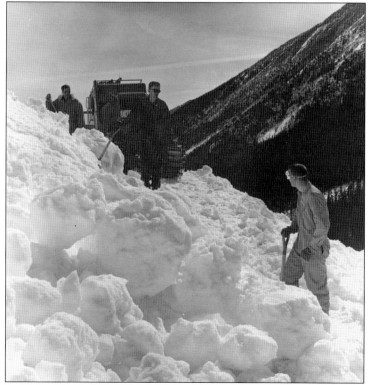

Here a Tucker Sno-Cat and Ski-do are at the site of another Mount Chapin avalanche in March 1968. The picture was taken by park naturalist Robert J. Haines. Colorado leads the nation in avalanche fatalities each year. Access roads into Rocky Mountain National Park are kept open in winter. There is much less risk of avalanche for cross-country skiers in the lower Wild Basin area of the park.

103

In this photograph taken on March 11, 1935, wind damage is apparent at Civilian Conservation Corps Camp NP-4-C in Hollowell Park. High winds and sudden blizzards are more common on the east side than the west side of Rocky Mountain National Park. A close look at the twisted trees at tree line reveals the effects of snow and winds that often reach in excess of 100 miles per hour.

This photograph shows damage from a blow down at Hidden Valley in 1973. On November 29, 2007, during a windstorm, the top of a beetle-killed tree broke off and came down across the Sandbeach trail in the Wild Basin area of the park, falling on two hikers. One man was injured and the other killed when he struck his head on a rock after being hit by the falling tree.

On the last day of July 1976, a thunderstorm lingered for four hours over the Big Thompson Canyon. Twelve inches of rain fell between 6:30 and 10:30 p.m., triggering a massive flood. There was no National Weather Service warning, and only 20 percent of the endangered residents were notified by knocks on the door. At the time, an estimated 2,500 to 3,500 visitors and residents packed the shops and summer houses.

People in homes and motels who did not heed flood warnings found themselves clinging to mattresses that floated toward the ceiling. Many broke through the roof or waited it out in attic crawl spaces or clung to chimneys and rooftops. Others spent the night in the tops of trees. Some in structures like the one pictured here were swept away in the early hours of August 1, 1976.

As people celebrated the state's centennial that weekend, the shops and cafes along the canyon road between Loveland and Estes Park were crowded. In this photograph, an antique store was partially destroyed during the Big Thompson flood. At the mouth of the canyon, the rate of flow went from 165 cubic feet per second to 31,200 cubic feet per second, sweeping away almost everything in its path.

Some were lucky. Guests at the Glen Haven Inn were aware of heavy rain and noticed when the electricity went off, but they did not learn until the next morning that the town hall across the street had floated off its foundations or that their cars in the parking lot were buried in silt to their windows. This photograph shows a vehicle that washed away during the Big Thompson flood.

This demolished car rests on the bank after the Big Thompson flood. One hundred forty-five people lost their lives in the flood. It was the worst natural disaster to ever occur in Colorado. The flood destroyed 418 homes and damaged another 138, and wiped out 52 businesses. A main source of the floodwater was the North Fork of the Big Thompson, which originates in Rocky Mountain National Park.

The Lawn Lake Dam broke early in the morning in July 1982. An observer of the wall of water that came rushing down the Roaring River in Rocky Mountain National Park called park personnel who were able to alert 275 campers before floodwaters engulfed the Aspenglen Campground 75 minutes later. This sign in a picture taken in July 1982 shows the debris littered on the campground road.

Five miles downstream from the broken dam, floodwaters reached Horseshoe Park where the Roaring Fork runs into the Fall River. The waters deposited a fan of debris, shown here in this 1982 photograph. Waters reaching the wide mountain valley slowed somewhat as they spread out in the meadow. When the bowl-like meadow overflowed, the waters rushed on toward Aspenglen Campground.

The Lawn Lake Dam was an earthen structure built in 1903 and held back as much as 219,724,000 gallons of water. After the flood, inspectors determined that the probable cause of the failure was deterioration in the lead caulking used between the outlet pipe and gate valves. Flood devastation to structures in its path along the lower Fall River is shown in this July 14, 1982, photograph.

The floodwaters from the Lawn Lake Dam break traveled 12.2 miles in 3.2 hours to reach Estes Park at 8:12 a.m. The aftermath in the town is revealed in this 1982 photograph. In addition to the loss of three lives, the flood is estimated to have caused $31 million in public and private damage. Of 103 business owners on Elkhorn Avenue, 64 gave up and moved away.

Two Rocky Mountain National Park campgrounds take reservations. Others operate on a first come, first served basis. Park pamphlets remind people that this is black bear country and warn campers to use food storage lockers. Bear attacks, though infrequent, can be deadly. This photograph taken July 25, 1971, shows the site of a bear attack. The tent was torn from the tree, and half the tent stakes were pulled out.

The canvas shown in this picture reveals canine fang punctures from a bear that attacked a site in the Holzwarth campground. The same canine marks were found in a four-inch foam mattress at the site. It is rare for bears to be aggressive toward humans in Rocky Mountain National Park. In all of North America in the 20th century, there were only 52 recorded deaths from black bears.

Trained dogs are sometimes used for search-and-rescue missions or to track dangerous animals that have attacked humans in Rocky Mountain National Park. Aggressive bears are sometimes trapped in barrel-shaped steel cages. When dogs are needed to search for missing hikers, the Front Range Rescue dogs and the Larimer County Search and Rescue dogs are often called in to assist park staff.

When a bear becomes a nuisance and a danger in Rocky Mountain National Park, attempts are sometimes made to trap the bear so it can be relocated. This photograph was taken by assistant superintendent John S. McLaughlin in July 1930. It shows the release of a bear from a steel trap.

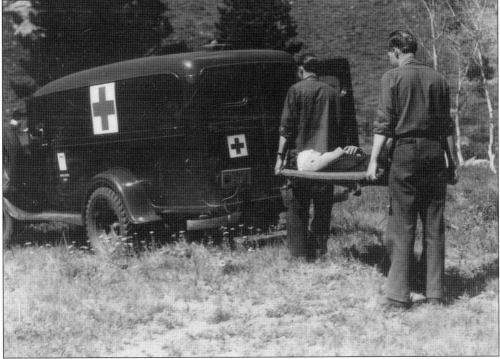

Dangers more common to people than animal attacks are getting lost or falling and requiring medical assistance. In this picture taken by a Civilian Conservation Corps education advisor in July 1938, a rescue mission is carried out. When a search mission is not immediately successful, others who join the park staff include Larimer County Search and Rescue, Grand County Search and Rescue, and the Rocky Mountain Rescue Group.

Trained personnel must be ready to render services at all seasons of the year. This photograph taken in 1971 by park naturalist Robert J. Haines shows winter rescue training taking place at Glacier Gorge Junction. Members of rescue teams spend an average of 100 hours annually training to maintain their skills and expertise. They may be called out to rescue skiers, snowmobilers, snowshoers, and climbers.

J. Herbert Hegler, a seasonal naturalist in Rocky Mountain National Park, took this photograph in August 1956 of a helicopter rescue from Mount Craig. Helicopters can carry rescuers to backcountry sites, conduct aerial searches, and carry out victims. Helicopters used in recent searches included a Bell 407 helicopter from Western Area Power Authority (WAPA). The WAPA helicopter is equipped with an infrared device used for its heat-seeking capability.

Eight

NATURAL BEAUTIES

Rocky Mountain National park is open all year. Whatever season someone is fortunate enough to visit, he or she will be struck by its beauty. In spring, there will still be snow on the ground as well as on the majestic peaks. In summer, the meadows are filled with wildflowers, and the campgrounds are busy with visitors. Fall brings a special season of color and sound when numerous aspen glow in golden and orange colors. In September and October, the bull elks bugle to their herds in Horseshoe Meadow. And in winter, one may see the tracks of the snowshoe hare and coyotes as well as the tracks of cross-country skiers and snowshoers.

Much can be seen by the visitor who only has time to drive through the park and over Trail Ridge Road. Numerous birds and animals may be observed, including massive elk, mule deer, marmots, and pika. The gray jay greets visitors at almost every overlook hoping for a handout. The Kawuneechee Visitor Center, the Beaver Meadows Visitor Center, the Fall River Visitor Center, and the Alpine Visitor Center provide knowledgeable staff to answer questions. The Moraine Park Museum has interactive exhibits, and a glimpse into the past is available at the Holswarth Historic Site.

Those who can stay long enough to hike some of the numerous trails or camp in one of the five park campgrounds will see clear streams, rushing waterfalls, squirrels, songbirds, and maybe an owl toward dusk. They may attend one of the ranger-led programs. Even short hikes will provide views of Lily Lake, Bear Lake, and Sprague Lake. Longer treks will lead the outdoor enthusiastic to the top of Flattop Mountains and the opportunity to view distant peaks. The experienced climber may venture to the top of Longs Peak or even try a technical climb. Those in good condition and who plan ahead may get a permit to backpack and spend the night at one of the many permitted high country sites. Visitors should enjoy the beauties of the park in their own way for as much time as they have.

Directly in the center of this 1930 picture, taken by park photographer George A. Grant, is Longs Peak, which at 14,259 feet is the highest mountain in Rocky Mountain National Park. Its first recorded sighting was by Maj. Stephen Long's party on a scouting expedition in 1820. The first recorded successful climb of the peak was made on August 23, 1868, by John Wesley Powell and six other men.

This photograph shows Longs Peak from Flattop Mountain. Flattop, Hallett, and Otis Peaks are close enough to be climbed in the same day. A trail leads north from Bear Lake to Flattop, which is on the Continental Divide. The 4.5-mile Flattop Trail switches back and forth to the top of the mountain. This trail affords great views of Bierstadt, Dream, and Emerald Lakes.

This shows Chasm Lake and the east face of Longs Peak. Lacking technical experience and equipment to make a rescue if needed, the National Park Service at first refused requests to climb the Diamond on the east face of the peak. Once it was opened to climbing, David Rearick and Robert Kamps got a permit and made the first ascent of the Diamond on Longs Peak on August 1, 1960.

Alpine sunflowers brighten this meadow. Different ecosystems in the park are home to a wide variety of plants. The alpine zone, with its brief growing season, produces many low-growing mat and cushion plants. Alpine avens put down deep roots to grow on the tundra. In the sub-alpine are broom huckleberry, junipers, and twinflower, while growing in the montane are chokecherry, wax currant, and service berry.

Above Black Lake near the head of Glacier Gorge are, from left to right, Longs Peak, Keyboard of the Winds, Pagoda Peak, and the Spearhead in this photograph taken by ranger Al Rozum. The elevation of Black Lake is 10,600 feet. The Keyboard of the Winds is a collection of pinnacles in the ridge. The lowest of the Keys in the Keyboard of the Winds is at 12,700 feet.

Frederick E. Chapin took this photograph of Mary's Lake in 1900. Mary's Lake is located just outside of what is now Rocky Mountain National Park near the town of Estes Park. In 1861, it was named for Mary L. Fleming, the bride of Milton Estes, whose father, Joel Estes, was the first settler in Estes Park. Today Mary's Lake is a reservoir in the Big Thompson Project.

This 1920 photograph shows hikers viewing Mills Lake and Glacier Gorge. Sitting at 9,940 feet of elevation in a rocky basin, Mills Lake provides great views to the south of Longs Peak, Pagoda Mountain, and Chief's Head Peak. The lake, which is less than three miles from the Glacier Gorge Trailhead, was named for naturalist Enos Mills.

Ranger Jerome Kasten took this photograph of visitors at Bear Lake in 1960. The .5-mile loop trail along the lakeshore of Bear Lake is the most visited trail in Rocky Mountain National Park. Bear Lake has an elevation of 9,475 feet and is located in the heart of the park beneath Hallett Peak and the Continental Divide.

Dream Lake, the most frequently photographed lake in Rocky Mountain National Park, was named by George Barnard, who led several outings for the Colorado Mountain Club. Barnard assisted the Colorado Geographic Board in finding names for park features. He named this lake in 1913, during the second annual outing of the newly formed club. Dream Lake is located at an elevation of 9,880 feet.

This 1889 photograph taken by F. E. Chapin shows one of the many waterfalls found in Rocky Mountain National Park. This beautiful spot was named Marguerite Falls by Dr. William J. Workman, an avid fisherman, who built the Fern Lake Lodge. One of Dr. Workman's visitors was Marguerite Turk from Denver. The Turks were a prominent Colorado family with roots in Central City.

Alberta Falls is a popular hiking destination less than a mile from the Glacier Gorge Trailhead on the Bear Lake road. Abner Sprague, an early settler in the Estes Park area, named the waterfall in this photograph after his wife. Alberta Falls carries the roaring waters of Glacier Creek. Along the trail are several pools and small cataracts. Near the falls are many logs and burned stumps. Hundreds of acres of the forest in this area were burned by a forest fire that swept through in 1900. The trail continues south to a sign marking a fork. Along the way to the fork in the trail, a left turn leads hikers up a steep path to the Boulder Field, located on the side of Longs Peak. At the fork, one branch in the trail leads into Glacier Gorge and Mills Lake while the other goes to Loch Vale. Below the falls, Glacier Creek flows past Sprague Lake and on to the Big Thompson River.

The area that is now Rocky Mountain National Park felt the effects of the Ice Age. Glaciation in the park probably started 1.6 millions years ago. Today the park has several small glaciers and permanent snowfields, including Andrews Glacier, Sprague Glacier, Tyndall Glacier, Taylor Glacier, Rowe Glacier, Mills Glacier, and Moomaw Glacier. Taylor Glacier is shown here in a 1956 photograph taken by chief naturalist Norman Herkenham.

Pictured are "seracs," or blocks of ice that are formed by intersecting small crevasses, seen here on Rowe Glacier in a photograph by F. E. Chapin taken in 1888. Rowe Glacier lies on the southeast side of Rowe Peak, north of Hagues Peak. The round-trip walk to Rowe Glacier begins at the Lawn Lake Trail from Horseshoe Park.

Elk were plentiful in the Rocky Mountain National Park area but were hunted almost to extinction. A small transplant herd brought from Wyoming increased to about 3,000 elk. Park officials have prepared a plan to cull the herd through hunting to a sustainable population of about 1,600 to 2,100 elk. This photograph shows a bull elk. Fully grown animals weigh around 700 pounds and feed on aspen and willow stands.

This picture of mule deer in Rocky Mountain National Park was taken in 1963 by Roger Contor, park superintendent. Mule deer, common in the western half of North America, get their name from their long mule-like ears. On average, males weigh 150 to 300 pounds and females average 100 to 175 pounds. Mule deer have black-tipped tails, and they move by bounding on all four feet.

These bighorn sheep on McGregor Mountain in Rocky Mountain National Park were photographed in 1936 by ranger Merlin K. Potts. Males, called rams, are famous for curved horns and may grow to exceed 30 pounds. Females, or ewes, weigh up to 200 pounds. Their horns are smaller with only slight curvature. Rocky Mountain bighorn sheep have brown and white coats with a dark line that runs down their spines.

Enos Mills, often called the father of Rocky Mountain National Park, took this picture of a bighorn sheep in 1919. Bighorn sheep weigh between 115 and 280 pounds and are 50 to 62 inches long, with a shoulder height of 32 to 40 inches. The rams that have horns weighing as much as 30 pounds sometimes take part in head-to-head combat. They live 10 to 15 years.

This picture of a beaver was taken by ranger Merlin K. Potts in 1936. Beaver are semi-aquatic animals. Adults weigh over 40 pounds and are about 3 feet long. Beavers mate for life, and both parents help care for young. Favorite foods are lily bulbs and bark from aspen. Beavers swim with their webbed hind feet.

Snowshoe hare tracks show in this photograph taken in 1940 by ranger H. Raymond Gregg. This medium-sized rabbit gets its name from its long hind feet with toes that can be spread out like snowshoes. The snowshoe hare exchanges its thin brown summer coat for a heavy white fluffy winter coat. Because of its changing color, which makes for excellent seasonal camouflage, it is sometimes called a varying hare.

The gray jay, also known by the names of Canada jay, Camp Robber, and Whiskey Jack, is a medium-sized bird, mostly colored in shades of gray, and common below timberline. It is 10 to 13 inches long. Jays are seldom found alone. These birds are very tame and aggressively beg for illegal handouts. They are frequent uninvited picnic guests. This photograph was taken by Robert J. Haines in July 1967.

The Clark's nutcracker is found near timberline. It is 12 to 13 inches long and has a gray body with contrasting black and white on wings and tail. It has a long bill used for eating pine seeds. The Clark's nutcracker is wary of people but will welcome opportunities to sample human foods.

The white-tailed ptarmigan is a small grouse, 12 to 14 inches long. During summer, it resides on the tundra eating seeds, while it winters in the high forests eating nutritious willow buds. It rarely flies, depending instead on camouflage for safety. In summer, it is colored in mottled gray and brown, while in winter it is mostly white. In spring and fall, it is a mixture of brown and white.

Common in the park is the black-billed magpie. This picture taken by H. Raymond Gregg in 1938 shows the bird's very large nest. Magpies are about 18 inches in length with sturdy black beaks and dark legs. They have black heads, breasts, rumps, and under-tails with white bellies and white patches on the wing that show in flight. Magpies eat insects and carrion.

The great horned owl is a large bird, 18 to 25 inches tall, and is fairly common at lower elevations though rarely seen since it is nocturnal. The great horned owl is a mottled gray and brown with ear tufts and yellow eyes. It preys mainly on small rodents but will eat larger animals such as hares, skunks, and hawks. This photograph was taken by naturalist C. O. Harris in 1960.

BIBLIOGRAPHY

Abbott, Carl, Stephen J. Leonard, and Thomas J. Noel. Colorado: A History of the Centennial State. Boulder, CO: University Press of Colorado, 2005.

Arps, Louisa Ward, and Elinor Eppich Kingery. High Country Names: Rocky Mountain National Park and Indian Peaks. Boulder, CO: Johnson Books, 1994.

Buchholtz, C. W. Rocky Mountain National Park. Boulder, CO: Colorado Associated University Press, 1983.

Bueler, William. M. Roof of the Rockies: A History of Mountaineering in Colorado. Boulder, CO: Pruett Publishing Company, 1974.

estes.on-line.com/rmnp/articles/briefhis.html

Kaye, Glen. Guide to Holzwarth Trout Lodge Historic Site Estes Park, CO: Rocky Mountain Nature Association: Rocky Mountain National Park, 2003.

Lamb, Elkanah. Past Memories and Future Thoughts. United Brethren Publishing House, 1903.

Marsh, Charles. People of the Shining Mountain. Boulder, CO: Pruett Publishing Company, 1982.

Perry, Phyllis J. It Happened in Rocky Mountain National Park. Guilford, CT: Globe Pequot Press, 2008.

Wood, Richard E. Here Lies Colorado: Fascinating Figures in Colorado History. Helena, MT: Farcountry Press, 2005.

DISCOVER THOUSANDS OF LOCAL HISTORY BOOKS FEATURING MILLIONS OF VINTAGE IMAGES

Arcadia Publishing, the leading local history publisher in the United States, is committed to making history accessible and meaningful through publishing books that celebrate and preserve the heritage of America's people and places.

Find more books like this at
www.arcadiapublishing.com

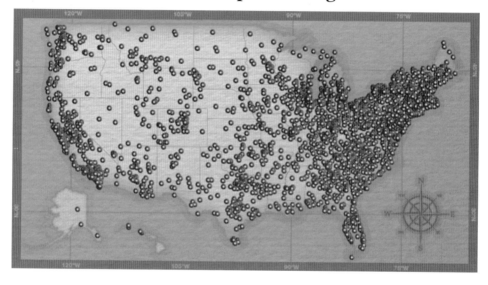

Search for your hometown history, your old stomping grounds, and even your favorite sports team.

Consistent with our mission to preserve history on a local level, this book was printed in South Carolina on American-made paper and manufactured entirely in the United States. Products carrying the accredited Forest Stewardship Council (FSC) label are printed on 100 percent FSC-certified paper.

MADE IN THE